Win the Cup!

by Rachel Russ
Illustrated by Bill Ledger

Tricky words to practise before reading this book:

was, story

OXFORD

UNIVERSITY PRESS

In this story ...

Slink

Slink can kick.

Jin

Ben

Pip

3

"I will win the cup," Ben boasts.

Ben is too fast.

"I will win the cup," Jin boasts.

Jin floats up.

He is too high!

"I will win the cup," Pip boasts.

Pip trips up.

I will help her.

Slink spins.

He taps his feet.

tap
tap

Slink twists his tail.

swish
swish

Slink wins the cup!

15

Retell the story ...

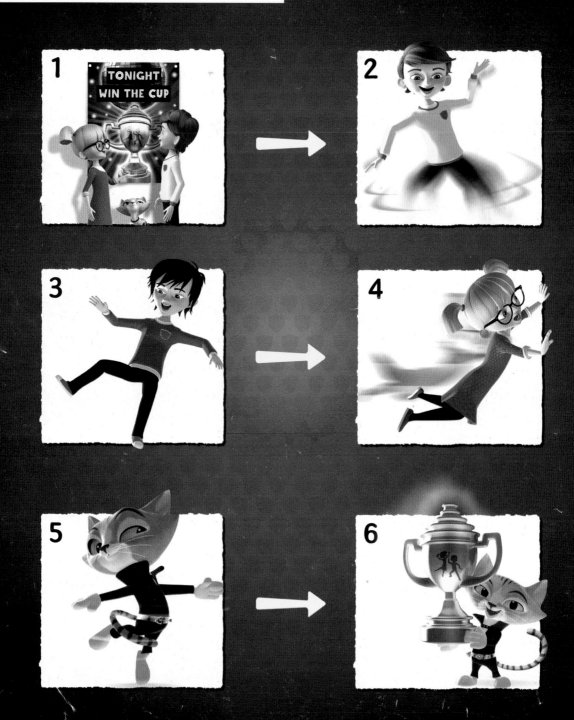